Macmillan/McGraw-Hill

Online Interactive Student Book

Treasures

www.macmillanmh.com

LOG ON ▶ **StudentWorks** *Plus*™
Interactive Student Book

D0579343

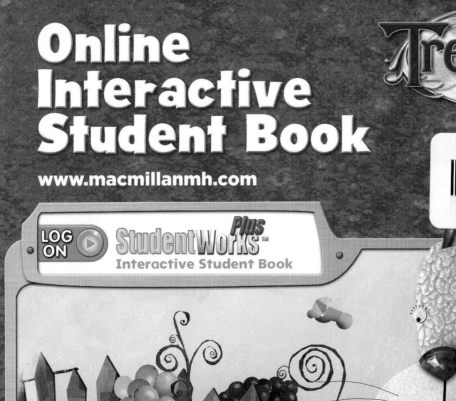

VIEW IT 👁
- Preview weekly concepts and selections

READ IT 📖
- Word-by-Word Reading

LEARN IT 🪐
- Comprehension Questions
- Research and Media Activities
- Grammar, Spelling, and Writing Activities

FIND OUT 🖱
- Summaries and Glossary in other Languages

LOG ON ▶ **Online Activities**
www.macmillanmh.com

- **Interactive activities** and **animated lessons** for guided instruction and practice

IWB Interactive White Board Ready!

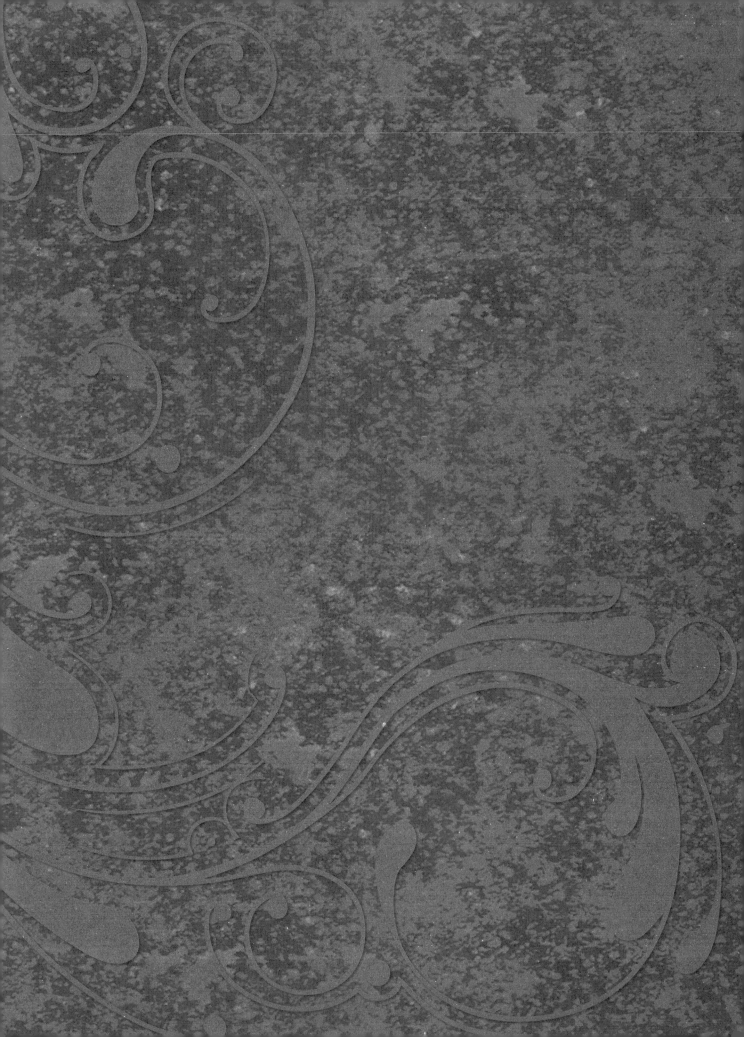

A Reading/Language Arts Program

 **Macmillan/McGraw-Hill**

Contributors

Time Magazine, Accelerated Reader

Students with print disabilities may be eligible to obtain an accessible, audio version of the pupil edition of this textbook. Please call Recording for the Blind & Dyslexic at 1-800-221-4792 for complete information.

B

The *McGraw-Hill* Companies

Mc Graw Hill Macmillan/McGraw-Hill

Published by Macmillan/McGraw-Hill, of McGraw-Hill Education, a division of The McGraw-Hill Companies, Inc., Two Penn Plaza, New York, New York 10121.

Printed in the United States of America

ISBN: 978-0-02-201729-3
MHID: 0-02-201729-1

2 3 4 5 6 7 8 9 DOW 13 12 11 10

Treasures

A Reading/Language Arts Program

Program Authors

Diane August
Donald R. Bear
Janice A. Dole
Jana Echevarria
Douglas Fisher
David Francis
Vicki Gibson
Jan E. Hasbrouck
Scott G. Paris
Timothy Shanahan
Josefina V. Tinajero

Macmillan/McGraw-Hill

Science

Nature Watch

The **Big** Question

What can we learn about the world of nature?

LOG ON ▶ VIEW IT

Theme Video
Nature Watch
www.macmillanmh.com

What can we learn about the world of nature?

The world of nature is all around us. It is up in the sky, in the trees, and under the ground. Plants, animals, the sky, water, and sunshine are all part of nature. There are lots of things to study in nature. You can study the night sky. You can learn about the weather and what makes a day sunny or rainy. You can study animals and why they do the things they do. Learning about nature can help us understand the world better.

Research Activities

Think of a plant or an animal you want to research. Use books and other sources of information. Include writing, diagrams, charts, or other visual aids. Share your report with the class.

Keep Track of Ideas

As you read, keep track of what you are learning about the world of nature on the **Accordion Foldable**. You may want to include the weather, seasons, animals, plants, earth, and sky.

FOLDABLES®
Study Organizer

Weather Seasons Animals Plants The Sky The Earth

Digital Learning

LOG ON ▶ **FIND OUT** www.macmillanmh.com

StudentWorks Plus
Interactive Student Book

- **Research Roadmap**
  Follow a step-by-step guide to complete your research project.

Online Resources

- Topic Finder and Other Research Tools
- Videos and Virtual Field Trips
- Photos and Drawings for Presentations
- Related Articles and Web Resources
- Web Site Links

People and Places

Carlsbad Caverns

Carlsbad Caverns are known around the world. They feature rooms with unique formations such as the Lake of the Clouds and the Hall of the White Giant. The Bat Cave is home to up to 16 species of bat.

In the Sky

Talk About It

What can you see when you look up at the sky?

LOG ON VIEW IT

Oral Language Activities
In the Sky
www.macmillanmh.com

poor
through
climbed
another
full
leaped
lucky

———

h<u>er</u>
f<u>ir</u>st

Read to Find Out
What happens when Lily Rat goes out at night?

 **LEARN IT**

Comprehension
www.macmillanmh.com

8

Lucky Lily

"Rats should not go out," the rats said. "We just saw Ralph, the cat."

But Lily Rat felt so hungry. "**Poor** me!" she sighed.

She peeked **through** her hole. She saw a hunk of cheese on the shelf. It looked so good!

She ran out and **climbed** up the shelf. First she had one bite of cheese. Then she had **another**. As she ate, she looked at the bright lights in the night sky. It was so pretty!

At last she felt **full**. She **leaped** off the shelf and ran home.

What a night!

"I am a **lucky** rat," Lily said.

Comprehension

Genre
Fiction is a story with made-up characters and events.

Ask Questions
Cause and Effect
Use your Cause and Effect Chart.

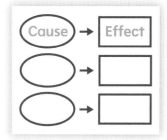

Read to Find Out
What happens when Kitten sees the moon?

Kitten's First Full Moon

written and illustrated by
KEVIN HENKES

Award
Winning
Author/
Illustrator

It was Kitten's first full moon.

When she saw it, she thought,

There's a little bowl of milk in the sky.

And she wanted it.

So she closed her eyes
and stretched her neck
and opened her mouth and licked.

But Kitten only ended up
with a bug on her tongue.
Poor Kitten!

Still, there was the little bowl

of milk, just waiting.

So she pulled herself together

and wiggled her bottom

and sprang from the top step of the porch.

But Kitten only tumbled—
bumping her nose and banging her ear
and pinching her tail.
Poor Kitten!

Still, there was the little bowl

of milk, just waiting.

So she chased it—

down the sidewalk,

through the garden,

past the field,

and by the pond.

But Kitten never seemed to get

closer.

Poor Kitten!

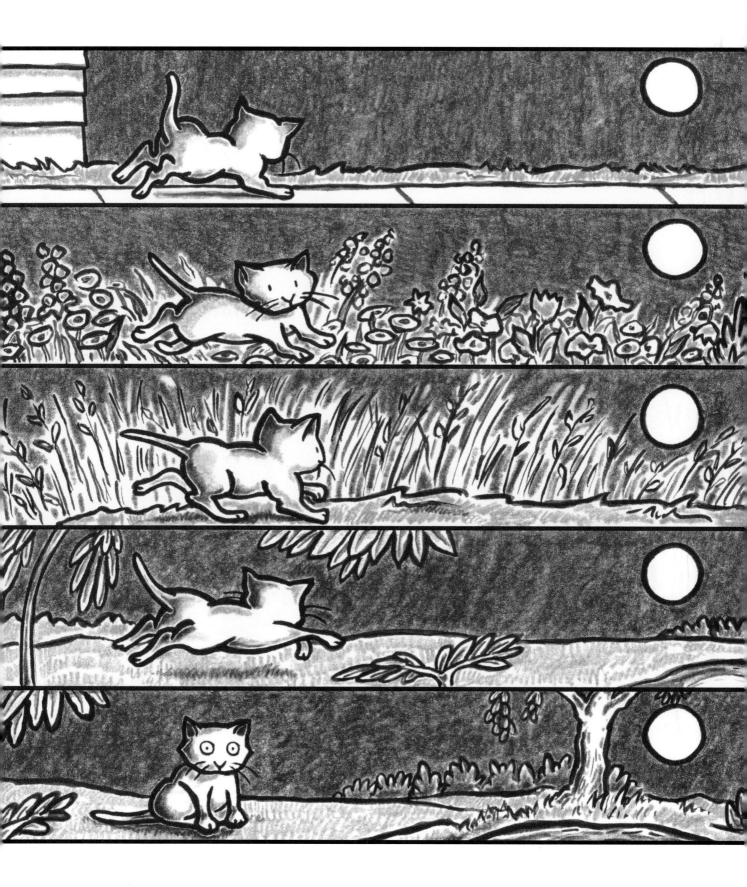

Still, there was the little bowl

of milk, just waiting.

So she ran
to the tallest tree
she could find,
and she **climbed**
and climbed
and climbed
to the very top.

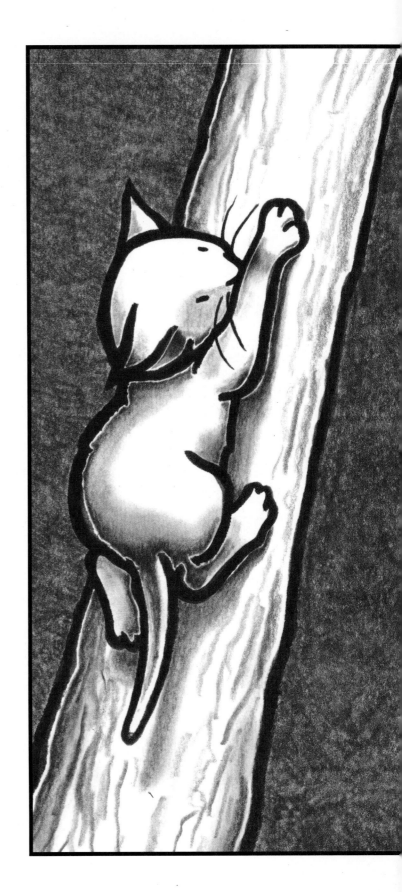

But Kitten
still couldn't reach
the bowl of milk,
and now she was
scared.
Poor Kitten!
What could she do?

Then, in the pond, Kitten saw
another bowl of milk.
And it was bigger.
What a night!

So she raced down the tree and

raced through the grass

and raced to the edge of the pond.

She leaped with all her might—

Poor Kitten!

She was wet and sad and tired

and hungry.

So she went

back home—

and there was

a great big

bowl of milk

on the porch,

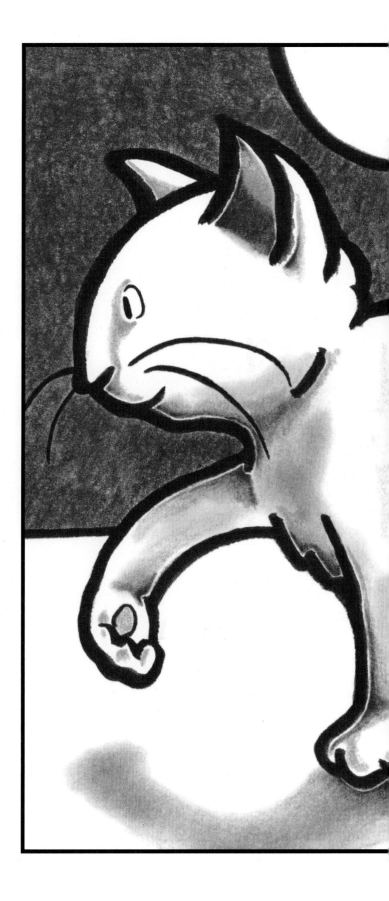

just waiting for her.

Lucky Kitten!

Kevin and Kitten

Kevin Henkes got the idea for *Kitten's First Full Moon* from a story he had begun to write many years before. Although he never finished this story, there was a line that read, "The cat thought the moon was a bowl of milk." He couldn't get this line out of his head, and slowly over the years the story of *Kitten's First Full Moon* formed.

Other books by Kevin Henkes

LOG ON ▶ FIND OUT
Author Kevin Henkes
www.macmillanmh.com

✔ Author's Purpose

Kevin Henkes got his story idea from a line he liked. Can you think of a line from a rhyme or story that you like? Draw and write about it.

✅ Comprehension Check

Retell the Story

Use the Retelling Cards
to retell the story in order.

Retelling Cards

Think and Compare

1. What causes Kitten to tumble,
   bump her nose, and bang her
   ear? Cause and Effect

2. What happens after Kitten
   sees the bowl of milk in the
   pond? Sequence

3. Why does Kitten never catch the bowl of
   milk she is chasing? Draw Conclusions

4. How is Kitten like Lily in "Lucky Lily"?
   Read Across Texts

Cause	→	Effect
	→	
	→	

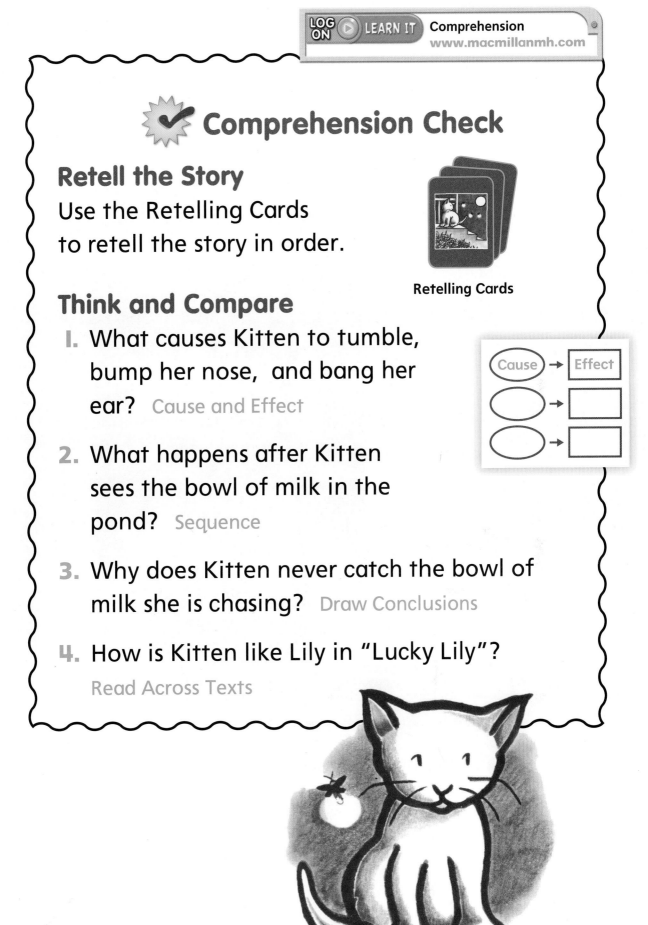

Ellen Ochoa IN SPACE

Ellen Ochoa is an **astronaut.** She has made many trips into space. Ellen lives in Houston, Texas. She works at the Johnson Space Center there.

Ellen thinks space trips are exciting. She likes seeing Earth from space. She sees our **planet** as the spacecraft rises through the sky. And she sees the moon and stars at night. What a thrilling sight that is!

Ellen works with a teammate inside a space module.

Ellen works a lot in space. She works with a team. Learning about space is a big job!

This is space food.
Ellen adds hot or cold
water to the pack.

In space, everything is **weightless**.
Everything floats!

So how can astronauts eat? Ellen has a tray
that sticks to her lap. Dried food and drinks
in packs stick to the tray. She eats tortillas, as
well. It is easy to stuff them with good things.

Ellen uses a sleeping bag like this one.
With straps like these, you can't fall out.

How can astronauts sleep if everything floats? They use sleeping bags that stick to the side of the spacecraft. They just float into the bag and strap themselves in. Then it is time to curl up and sleep tight!

Ellen Ochoa is dressed for space.

Ellen worked hard to be an astronaut. She went to college. She learned a lot of math and science. Then she went to school to learn about space flight. She had to pass a lot of tests. At last she became an astronaut. Ellen thinks that she has a fantastic job! Do you think so, too?

✔ Connect and Compare

- What do you think Kitten in *Kitten's First Full Moon* might do in a space module?

- What do the captions tell you about the pictures?

Write a Sky Poem

Writing

✔ Adjectives

An **adjective** is a word that tells more about a person, place, or thing.

Julie wrote a poem about the night sky.

The Night Sky
At night, the sky is black.
But look! Tiny golden dots!
I like the sky at night.
It is dark and light.

Your Turn

Think about the sky in the day or at night.

What does it look like?

What does it make you think?

Write a poem about the sky.

Grammar and Writing

- Read Julie's poem.
  Point to the adjectives that tell what the sky looks like.
  Find and name each punctuation mark.

- Check your poem.
  Do you include adjectives to describe the sky?
  Do you use punctuation marks correctly?

- Read your poem to a partner.

What Scientists Do

Talk About It

What is a scientist? What kinds of questions do scientists ask?

LOG ON ▶ VIEW IT

Oral Language Activities
What Scientists Do
www.macmillanmh.com

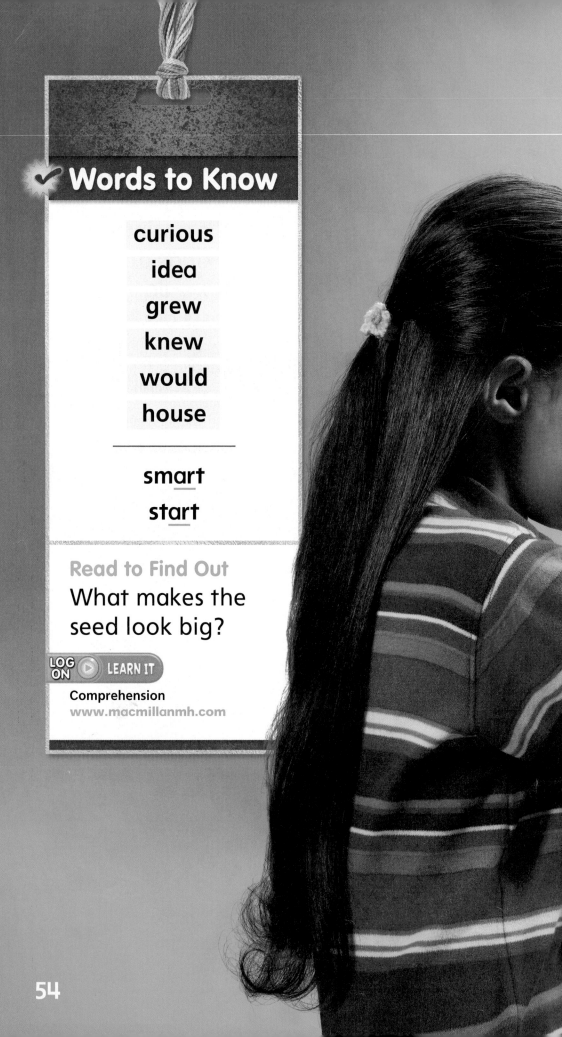

Words to Know

curious
idea
grew
knew
would
house

———

sm<u>ar</u>t
st<u>ar</u>t

Read to Find Out
What makes the
seed look big?

LOG ON ▶ LEARN IT

Comprehension
www.macmillanmh.com

54

Be Curious

Are you **curious**? Do you like to look at tiny things? Then try this smart **idea**.

Fill a bowl or glass with water. Then put something very little in your hand. Start with any tiny thing. This girl has a seed.

Next, place your hand at the back of the bowl or glass. Does the tiny thing look like it **grew**? I bet you **knew** it **would**.

Try this with more things at your **house**. They will look bigger, too!

Comprehension

Genre
A Biography is the true story of a person's life.

Ask Questions
✔ Make Inferences
Use your Inference Chart.

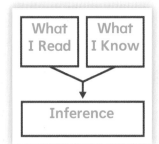

Read to Find Out
What makes Ben Franklin a great American?

Meet
Ben Franklin

by Philip Dray
illustrated by John Kanzler

Award
Winning
Author

Chapter 1

"Ben! Ben!" his friends called.

"Here I am," said Benjamin Franklin.

Ben was sitting on the docks. He was looking at the big ships. He liked the way the wind filled the sails.

Ben Franklin lived long ago. He liked to do many things. He liked to read. He was good at telling jokes and playing games.

Ben was a **curious** boy. He was smart, too.
He liked to dream. And he liked to make things.

One day, Ben made a red kite.

"This kite will be like the sails on the big ships,"
Ben said.

The next time Ben went swimming, he had his kite with him.

"What will you do with that?" his friends asked.

"You will see," said Ben.

Ben ran with the kite. The wind lifted it. He jumped in the water. He started to go fast. The kite was pulling him!

"Look at Ben go!" said his friends.

"How did Ben think of that?" they asked.

Chapter 2

Time went by. Ben **grew** up. He still liked to dream. He still liked to make things.

He made a new kind of stove. This stove was little, but it gave off lots of heat.

Ben made a new kind of glasses. They helped people to see up close and far away.

"How did Ben think of that?" people asked.

When Ben lived, people did not know much
about electricity.

Ben was curious about it. He **knew** it could
make sparks. He sometimes saw the sparks
when he put his key into a lock.

One day it was raining. Ben looked at a flash of lightning. It looked like a big spark. He wanted to know if that flash was electricity.

Chapter 3

"How can I find out if lightning is electricity?" Ben asked. "I can not go up in the sky."

Ben had an **idea**. A kite had helped him long ago. A kite could help him again.

"I can not get up there," he said. "But a kite can."

The next time it looked like rain, Ben
went out. The sky was dark. Ben had a
kite and an iron key. He sent the kite up.

Lightning flashed. Ben felt the kite string shake. He saw sparks of electricity jump off the key.

"This shows that lightning is electricity!" said Ben.

Ben had an idea. He knew that if lightning struck a **house**, it could catch on fire. He put an iron rod on top of his house.

"Lightning will strike the iron rod, but not my house," Ben said. "The rod will keep my house safe."

Ben's friends put up iron rods, too.
Today we still put them on our houses
so they will be safe.

Ben was glad that the lightning rods helped people. In his life, Ben Franklin **would** do many more things to help people. He had more things to dream about and more things to make.

Meet Philip Dray

Philip Dray says, "I write books about Americans who do brave things to make our country better. I wanted to tell the story of Ben Franklin and his kite because he had the courage to try something no one had ever tried before."

LOG ON ▶ FIND OUT

Author Philip Dray
www.macmillanmh.com

✔ Author's Purpose

Philip Dray wanted to write a true story about Ben Franklin and his new ideas. Write about one of Ben's inventions. Tell how it made life better.

✔ Comprehension Check

Retell the Selection

Use the Retelling Cards
to retell the selection in order.

Retelling Cards

Think and Compare

1. What did Ben Franklin want to know about lightning? Details

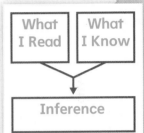

2. How did a kite help Ben? Retell

3. Why do you think Ben Franklin is a famous and honored American?
   Make Inferences

4. What did you learn to do in "Be Curious"? How is it like what Ben Franklin did? Read Across Texts

Genre
Nonfiction gives information about a topic.

✔ **Text Feature**
Bold Print points out important words.

Content Vocabulary
scientists
microscope
photograph

A Close Look

How do **scientists** see tiny things up close? They look through a **microscope.** That makes tiny things look big.

Look at the **photograph** in the circle.
It was taken with a microscope. It
shows things you see each day.
Can you tell what it is?

This is **salt**. Now you can see the
shape of each grain.

This is **hair**. You might have as many as 100,000 hairs on your head. Each hair has a hard coating.

This is a blade of **grass**.
Sharp edges help keep
bugs off.

What would you like to see close up?
What do you think it might look like?

Connect and Compare

What could young Ben Franklin have done with
a microscope?

✔ **Adjectives That Compare**

Add *-er* to adjectives that compare two. Add *-est* to compare three or more.

Write a Report

Kevin wrote about one of Ben Franklin's inventions.

Ben invented a lightning rod. He saw lightning burn a house. He put an iron rod on his roof. Lightning struck it and not the house. It was one of his greatest inventions.

Your Turn

Find out about one of
Ben Franklin's inventions.

Think about what the
invention does.

Write a report about why
it was important.

Grammar and Writing

- Read Kevin's report.
  What facts did you learn?
  Point to the adjective that compares.
  What does it end with?

- Check your report.
  Do you tell facts about the invention?
  Does the adjective that compares end
  correctly?

- Read your report to a partner.

Talk About It

What kinds of weather do you know about? What is your favorite kind of day?

What's the Weather?

Words to Know

warm
sound
their
extreme
predict
know
great

_____

st**or**m
f**or**

Warm and Cold Days

What is this day like? It is **warm** and wet. The rain makes a nice **sound**. Kids play in **their** homes.

This rain is **extreme**. But the storm will stop. Can you **predict** how the day will be then?

This day is cold. But these kids **know** how to stay warm. They run and jump and have a lot of fun. What a **great** day for playing!

Stormy Weather

How many sorts of storms do you know about?

There are all sorts of storms. Which storms do you see where you live?

On some days, the sky is gray. That might mean a storm is on the way.

A gray sky can mean a thunderstorm. You will see **great** flashes of lightning. Next comes a loud **sound**. That is a thunderstorm. It's time to go inside!

Lightning can make a tree catch fire.

Thunderstorms may have strong winds. The winds can blow branches off trees. Balls of ice may fall from the sky. This is hail. It can hail when it is **warm** or cold.

Most hail is small. Some is bigger than a tennis ball. ▷

Some storms come when it is very cold. It can snow so much that you can't see. Strong winds can blow snow into big piles. This is a blizzard.

A tornado can
destroy buildings. ▶

Some storms have **extreme** winds.
Tornadoes are made of fast winds that
spin and spin. The winds can pick up
trucks and homes.

Scientists have ways to **predict** when
tornadoes will come. Then people can
get out of **their** way.

What is the weather like today?
Does it look like a storm is on its
way? Or is it a great day for playing
outside?

 **Comprehension Check**

Tell What You Learned
What did you learn about storms?

Think and Compare

1. What is hail? Details

2. What can happen during a thunderstorm? Retell

3. How are a thunderstorm and a blizzard the same? How are they different? Compare and Contrast

4. How are the storms in "Stormy Weather" and "Warm and Cold Days" alike? Read Across Texts

Dangerous Storms

Some storms can be dangerous. Thunderstorms bring lightning. Lightning looks like a great flash in the sky. It can be dangerous.

You are not safe from lightning outside. You are not safe under a tree.

Where will you be safe from lightning? You will be safe inside. The best thing to do is get inside fast!

DIRECTIONS
Answer the questions.

1 Lightning looks like —

A trees swaying back and forth

B a great flash in the sky

C rain falling very fast

2 Why are thunderstorms dangerous?

A The rain will make you wet.

B The thunder is very loud.

C They bring lightning.

3 Where would you be safe from lightning?

A In your classroom

B On a river

C Under a tree

Write About the Weather

Rudy made a plan. Then he wrote a report about a tornado.

The writer included details about the storm.

TORNADOES

A tornado is a very strong kind of storm. It looks like a spinning cloud. The top of a tornado is in the sky. The bottom touches the ground. Tornadoes are dangerous.

Your Writing Prompt

Think about a storm you've seen or heard about.

Write a report about what this storm was like.

Writing Hints

 Give your report a title.

 Describe what the storm looked like and sounded like. Tell what the storm did.

 Check your report for mistakes.

97

The Seasons

Talk About It

What seasons do you have where you live? What is your favorite season?

Oral Language Activities
Seasons
www.macmillanmh.com

yellow

orange

against

wondered

below

fall

season

sure

___

n<u>ow</u>

sh<u>ou</u>ted

Read to Find Out

Why is fall a fun season?

LOG ON ▶ LEARN IT

Comprehension

www.macmillanmh.com

100

A Fun Season

"Let's play catch," said Liv.

"Now it's time to rake the leaves," said Dad.

Dad and Liv raked. There were red leaves, **yellow** leaves, and **orange** leaves.

Dad leaned his rake **against** a tree.

"Is it time for catch?" **wondered** Liv.

Then Dad started to run. He jumped up and landed in a big pile of leaves.

"Jump in, Liv!" Dad shouted.

Liv jumped as high as she could.

"Look out **below**!" she shouted.

"**Fall** is a fun **season**," said Dad.

"It **sure** is!" said Liv.

Comprehension

Genre
A **Fantasy** is a made-up story that could not really happen.

Summarize
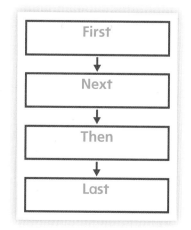 **Sequence**
Use your Sequence Chart.

First
↓
Next
↓
Then
↓
Last

Read to Find Out
What happens when Pinwheel discovers the leaves are falling?

Happy Fall!

from Pinwheel Days

by Ellen Tarlow • illustrated by Gretel Parker

Pinwheel was waiting for Squirrel.

"I like Squirrel and Squirrel likes me,"

he sang.

"Pinwheel! Be quiet!" came a voice.

"I am trying to sleep."

It was Owl.

"I am sorry, Owl," said Pinwheel.

Pinwheel felt an itch.

He rubbed **against** the tree.

"Pinwheel!" shouted Owl.

"Stop bumping the tree!

My bed is shaking."

"I am sorry, Owl," said Pinwheel.

Pinwheel stood as still as he could.

Something soft touched his head.

"What is that?" he **wondered**.

He shook his head.

A red leaf fell.

The wind blew.

More leaves fell.

"1, 2, 3, 4, 5," Pinwheel counted.

"Oh, no!" he said. "I broke the tree."

"Hello, Pinwheel," said Squirrel.
"Squirrel, I broke the tree!
Owl is going to be so mad at me!"
cried Pinwheel.

"Are you **sure** it's broken?"
asked Squirrel.

The wind blew.

More leaves fell.

"6, 7, 8, 9, 10," Pinwheel counted.

"See?" he said. "Broken."

"Very broken," said Squirrel.

They looked up.

More leaves fell.

"Go back!" they shouted.

But the leaves kept on falling.

Red leaves.

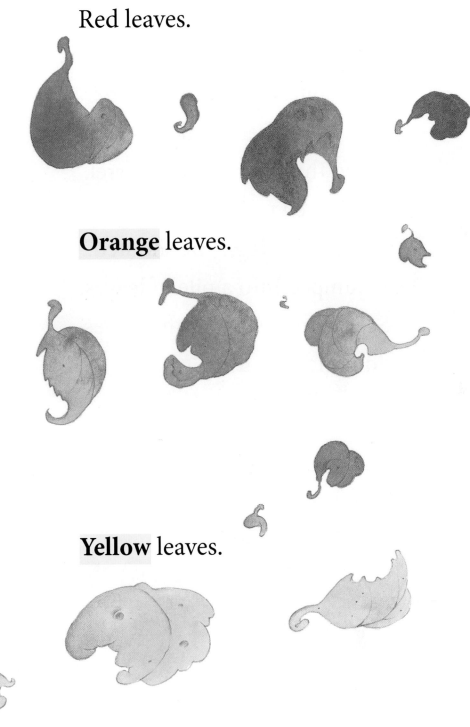

Orange leaves.

Yellow leaves.

There were too many to count.

"You won't like it down here,"
Pinwheel told the leaves.
"You will only get stepped on,"
said Squirrel.
"And squashed," added Pinwheel.
"Very squashed," said Squirrel.
"Let's show them," said Pinwheel.
"Good thinking," said Squirrel.
He climbed up the tree trunk.
"Look out **below**!" he shouted.
He jumped into a pile of leaves.
"See?" Pinwheel told the leaves.
"Squashed!"

Then he heard laughing.
"Pinwheel," laughed Squirrel.
"Jump in!"

Squirrel popped out of the leaves.
He jumped back in.

Then Pinwheel jumped in.
"Catch me!" called Squirrel.

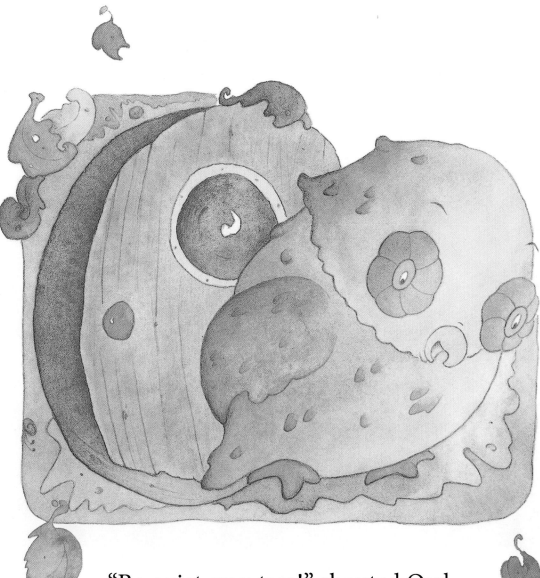

"Be quiet, you two!" shouted Owl.

He stepped out of his house.

He looked around.

"Ah, **fall**!" he said.

He looked down.

"Hide!" said Squirrel.

"Where?" asked Pinwheel.

"Look out below!" called Owl.

He jumped into the leaves.

"Run!" said Squirrel.

But it was too late.

"Hello," said Owl. "Happy fall!"

"Fall?" asked Pinwheel.

"Fall?" asked Squirrel.

"It's my favorite **season**," said Owl.
Pinwheel looked at the colorful
leaves.
"Happy fall!" he shouted as loudly
as he could.
Then he jumped in to find Squirrel.

Meet Pinwheel's Pals

Ellen Tarlow has always loved stories about talking animals. She got the idea for Pinwheel after seeing a photograph of a baby donkey.

Gretel Parker got her first real paint box when she was four. She has been painting animals ever since. Her favorite character in *Happy Fall!* is Owl, because "he looks a bit cross at first but is very kindhearted, really."

Another book by Ellen Tarlow and Gretel Parker

Pinwheel Days

By Ellen Tarlow
Art by Gretel Parker

LOG ON ▶ FIND OUT

Author Ellen Tarlow
Illustrator Gretel Parker
www.macmillanmh.com

✔ Author's Purpose

Ellen Tarlow got the idea for Pinwheel after seeing a donkey in a photograph. Make up a character based on an animal you have seen. Write about your character.

✔ Comprehension Check

Retell the Story

Use the Retelling Cards
to retell the story in order.

Retelling Cards

Think and Compare

1. What is Pinwheel doing at the beginning of the story? Details

2. What does Pinwheel think when the leaf first falls on his head? What happens next? Sequence

First
↓
Next
↓
Then
↓
Last

3. How do Pinwheel and Squirrel feel about Owl when he first comes out of his house? How do they feel at the end? What changed? Character

4. How do Pinwheel and Squirrel act like Liv and Dad in "A Fun Season"? Read Across Texts

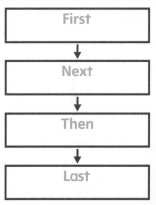

Genre
Nonfiction gives information about a topic.

✔ **Text Feature**
Some Diagrams show the order in which things happen.

Content Vocabulary
summer
winter
animals

LOG ON ▶ FIND OUT

Science Seasons
www.macmillanmh.com

SEASONS

A season is a time of year. There are four seasons in a year. They are spring, **summer**, fall, and **winter**.

In spring the weather gets warmer. The days stay light longer. It may rain a lot in spring. The sun and rain help plants grow. Many **animals** are born in spring. There is a lot for them to eat then.

In spring leaves on trees start to come out.

Summer comes after spring. Summer has the most daylight. That means more time to play outside! The weather gets hot in a lot of places. Plants grow big in summer. Animals eat and grow big, too.

In summer the leaves on trees get bigger.

Fall follows summer. There is less daylight in fall. The weather starts to get colder. Plants stop growing. Some animals save food for when it will get much colder. Other animals go where they will find more food.

In fall leaves may turn red, yellow, and orange.

In many places winter is cold. It may snow. There is not much that animals can eat. So some animals, such as bears, sleep in winter. These animals will wake up in spring when they can find food.

In winter trees have no leaves. They will grow again in spring.

Spring

Summer

Fall

Winter

Look at these trees. How do they change over a year? In which season do trees have the most leaves? The fewest?

Connect and Compare

- How do the pictures show the way seasons change over a year?

- What does the diagram tell you about seasons?

Write a Poem About a Season

Writing

✔ **Color Words and Number Words**

Color Words and Number Words are adjectives that tell more about a noun.

Ruby wrote a poem about spring.

In spring, the rain comes
Down, down, down!
But then flowers come up.
One flower, two flowers,
three flowers.
Red, yellow, pink flowers.
Flowers come up, up, up!

Your Turn

Write a poem about a season you like.

Tell something special that happens in that season.

Use words to describe how the season looks, feels, sounds, or smells.

Grammar and Writing

- Read Ruby's poem.
  Point to the color and number words.
  What do they tell more about?

- Check your poem.
  Did you tell how the season looks, feels, sounds, or smells?
  Did you use color and number words?

- Illustrate your poem and read it aloud.

Talk About It

How do baby animals change as they grow up?

Oral Language Activities
Watching Animals Grow
www.macmillanmh.com

Watching Animals Grow

cub

eyes

learn

open

enough

air

wild

_____

join

noise

Read to Find Out

How do bear cubs change as they get older?

Comprehension
www.macmillanmh.com

128

A Cub Grows Up

When a bear **cub** is born, its **eyes** are closed. But it does not need to see to eat. The tiny cub drinks milk. It does not need to **learn** how. It just knows how. Soon its eyes **open**. After a while, the cub is strong **enough** to go out in the fresh **air**.

Then it is time to join the others in the **wild**. The cub learns to hunt and catch fish. It must not make a noise. The cub also learns which parts of plants are best for eating.

Soon the cub will be grown up!

129

Comprehension

Genre

gives information about a topic.

Summarize

✓ Sequence

Use your Sequence Chart.

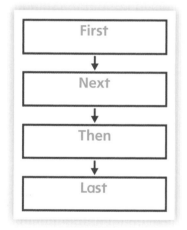

First

↓

Next

↓

Then

↓

Last

Read to Find Out

How does a tiger cub change as it grows up?

130

A Tiger Cub Grows Up

by Joan Hewett

photographs by
Richard Hewett

In the Nursery

Tara is a tiger **cub**.
She was born in a **wild** animal park.
The cub is hungry.
She feels the tip of the bottle.
She drinks her warm milk.

When Tara is
9 days old,
her **eyes** **open**.

Grown-up tigers like to swim. But little Tara
does not like her first bath.

Mary feeds Tara.
She talks to the tiger cub.
She gives her kisses.

At night, Mary takes the cub home with her.
Tara drinks her milk.
She falls asleep.

Then Tara wakes up.
She is hungry!
She wants more milk.

Tara drinks until her belly is full.
She falls back to sleep.
As she sleeps, she grunts
and squeals.

Tara is 3 weeks old.
Her baby teeth are coming in.
She has pointed teeth for tearing meat.

And she has rounded teeth for chewing.

Chewing feels good. But a plastic tray
is hard to hold with chubby paws.

Each day, Mary shows the cub a piece of meat.
Tara does not want to try it. Not yet!

Playtime is a time to **learn**.
Can Tara crawl over Mary's legs?
How hard will Mary let her bite?

Tara is 3 months old. Mary takes Tara to the animal doctor. It is time for a checkup.

The bright lights are scary. The tiger cub roars.

H-O-W-R-R

Tara Goes Outdoors

Tara is healthy. And she is old **enough** to play outside.

Grass and sky seem strange to Tara.
The **air** is filled with new smells.
The tiger cub follows her nose.
She runs across the grass.

Lynn takes care of Tara now.
Lynn hugs Tara. She plays with Tara.
She shows her falling leaves.

Lynn plays with Tara every day.
She teaches Tara what she can do.
She teaches Tara what she cannot do.

Tara greets Lynn with a friendly chuffing sound.
Lynn returns the greeting.

Climbing over Lynn is fun.
Following Lynn is fun.
Tara creeps along the ground.
Then she pounces!

Tara Joins the Grown-up Tigers

Tara is 9 months old. She is big and strong. She can join the park's grown-up tigers. Tara likes her new home. She can run across the grass. She can climb on logs. She can nap under leafy trees.

Tara watches the big tigers swim.
She walks around the pond. It is hot.
So Tara jumps in. Tara is 1 year old.
The tiger cub has grown up.

S·P·L·A·S·H

Watching Animals with the Hewetts

Joan Hewett thinks research is the most difficult, interesting, and fun part of writing. Many of her books are about baby animals living in zoos or rescue centers.

Richard Hewett says, "I think children's books are the best." He often takes photographs for books written by his wife, Joan Hewett.

Other books by the Hewetts

LOG ON ▶ **FIND OUT**

Author Joan Hewett
Illustrator Richard Hewett
www.macmillanmh.com

✔ **Author's Purpose**

Joan Hewett wanted to give information about a baby animal. Write about a baby animal you know. Tell how it changed as it grew.

✔ Comprehension Check

Retell the Selection

Use the Retelling Cards
to retell the selection in order.

Retelling Cards

Think and Compare

First
↓
Next
↓
Then
↓
Last

1. What happens when Tara is nine
   days old? Details

2. What is Tara like when she is just
   born? How does she change after
   that? What is she like when she is
   one year old? Sequence

3. What is this selection about?
   Why did the author write it?

   Author's Purpose

4. How are Tara and the cub
   in "A Cub Grows Up" alike?

   Read Across Texts

Poetry

Genre
A Poem uses words that sound good together.

✔ Literary Elements
Alliteration is when the same beginning sound is repeated in a group of words.

Sensory Language describes the way things look, sound, feel, taste, or smell.

LOG ON ▶ FIND OUT

Poetry Using Poetic Language
www.macmillanmh.com

Gray Goose

by Julie Larios

Gray mama goose
in a tizzy,
honk-honk-honking herself dizzy,
can't find her gosling,
she's honking and running,
webbed feet slapping,
all wild waddle,
her feathers a muddle,
splashing through puddles,
wings flapping…

Ah,
there's her gold baby,
all fuzz,
napping.

156

Connect and Compare

- How does the author use sensory language to describe the goose and her baby?

- What parts of this poem use alliteration?

Writing

Write About Vets

Writing

✔ **Prepositions**

Prepositions show how parts of a sentence are connected. They may tell where and when.

Chris wrote about why vets are important.

You should always take your pet to the vet. Even if your pet is not sick, you should take it for a check-up. First the vet will put your pet on a table. Then the vet will do tests. This is the best way you can help your pet stay well.

Your Turn

How does a vet take care of animals?

Why is it important to take a pet to the vet?

Write about what a vet does and why vets are important.

Grammar and Writing

- Read Chris's writing.
  Point to each preposition.
  Does it tell where or when?

- Check your writing.
  Do you tell why vets are important?
  Do you use prepositions correctly?
  Does each sentence begin with a capital letter and end with a punctuation mark?

- Read your writing to a partner.

Review

Compare and
    Contrast
Sequence
Compound Words
Chart
Bold Print

What Grasshopper Learned

Once upon a time there was a Grasshopper who played music all day long. "Will you play with me, Ant?" he asked.

"I don't have time for such things," said Ant. "I must find food for winter, and make my home."

"But it isn't cold yet," said Grasshopper. So he kept playing, while Ant worked hard.

One day there was a snowstorm. The snow swirled and the wind howled.

Ant had plenty of food and a cozy home. Grasshopper had nothing to eat. He was cold!

Ant gave Grasshopper a bit of corn. "I hope you learned your lesson," said Ant.

Grasshopper sighed. "Thank you, Ant!" he said. "I learned that I must plan ahead."

What Does the Weather Chart Say?

The weather is what it is like outside. It may be **hot, warm,** or **cold.** Can you see **sun, rain,** or **clouds?** Can you feel the **wind?**

A class made a weather chart. The pictures show what the weather was like on each day.

sun   rain   clouds

snow   wind

Use the pictures to read the weather chart.

1 What was the weather like on Monday?

2 When did it rain?

3 On which days do you think the class played outside?

4 Which day was good for flying kites?

Monday	Tuesday	Wednesday	Thursday	Friday
4	5	6	7	8

Word Study

Word Clues

- Read the sentence below.

  The ground was moist after the rain.

- Does moist mean almost the same thing as: crunchy, wet, or happy? What clues help you know the answer?

- Read this sentence. My cat depends on me to take care of her.

- What words help you know what depends means?

Comprehension

All About Ben Franklin

- Reread *Meet Ben Franklin* on page 56 with a partner. List things Ben did in his life.

- Is this story true or a fantasy? Talk about how you can tell whether it is true or not.

Phonics

Make and Read Words

- Begin with the word turn.

- Change u to o.

- Change t to c.

- Change c to th.

- Add y to the end.

- What words did you make?

Writing

Write About a Fable

- Reread "What Grasshopper Learned" on page 160.

- Do you ever feel like the ant or the grasshopper? Do you ever act like them?

- Write about it. Tell what you think of the two characters. Tell how you have acted or felt like either.

Glossary

What Is a Glossary?

A glossary can help you find the meanings of words. The words are listed in alphabetical order. You can look up a word and read it in a sentence. Sometimes there is a picture.

cub

planet

Sample Entry

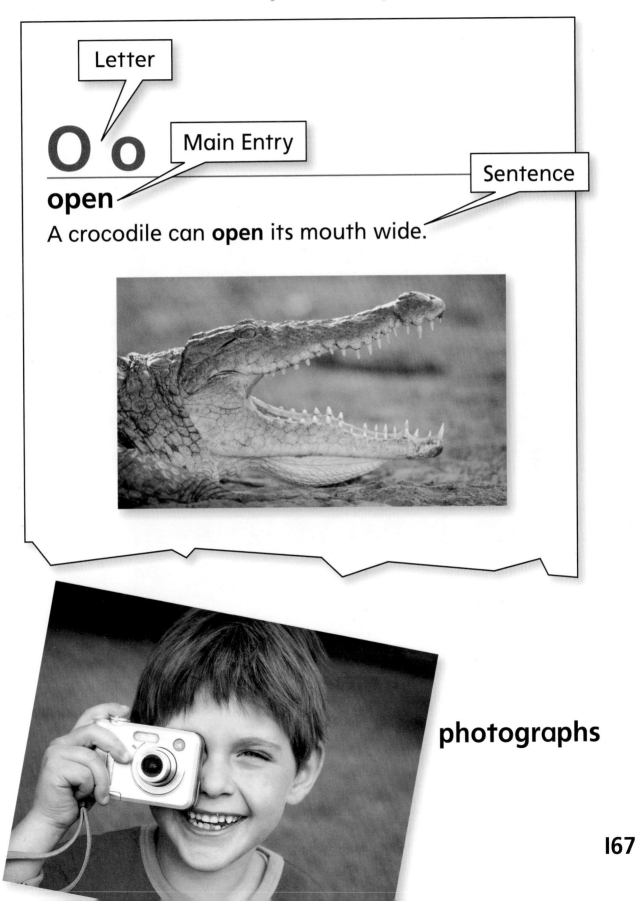

Letter

Main Entry

Sentence

O o

open

A crocodile can **open** its mouth wide.

photographs

Aa

against

The raindrops splashed **against** the window.

air

In the garden, the **air** smelled like flowers.

animals

Elephants are one of the biggest **animals**.

another

If there's no wind, we'll fly kites **another** day.

astronaut

An **astronaut** may travel to the moon.

Bb

below

From the airplane, the houses **below** looked tiny.

Cc

climbed

The squirrel **climbed** the tree.

cub

A lion **cub** stays near its mother.

curious

I am **curious** about polar bears.

Ee

enough

There was **enough** pizza for everyone.

extreme

A snowstorm is one kind of **extreme** weather.

eyes

This cat has yellow **eyes**.

Ff

fall

We like to watch the rain **fall**.

full

The pot is **full** of stew.

Gg

great

We had a **great** time at the park.

grew

Many plants **grew** in the garden.

Hh

house

I live in a red **house**.

Ii

idea

It's a good **idea** to wear your seat belt.

Kk

knew

I **knew** how to write my name when I was five.

know

Do you **know** how to whistle?

Ll

leaped

The rabbit **leaped** onto the rock.

learn

I want to **learn** about dinosaurs.

lucky

I feel **lucky** to have good friends.

Mm

microscope

Matt can see things up close with this **microscope**.

Oo

open

This crocodile can **open** his mouth wide.

orange

The pumpkin is a bright **orange** color.

Pp

photographs

Chris likes to take **photographs** with his new camera.

planet

Saturn is a **planet** with rings.

poor

The **poor** chipmunk ran from the swooping owl.

predict

The weather report may **predict** snow.

Ss

scientists

The **scientists** are working hard to discover new things.

season

Spring is the **season** when flowers start to bud.

sound

Thunder makes a loud **sound**.

summer

In **summer,** the lake is warm enough to swim in.

sure

Are you **sure** you fed the puppy?

Tt

their

My neighbors have **their** own swing set.

through

The sun peeked **through** the clouds.

Ww

warm

My new jacket is **warm**.

weightless

It would be fun to be **weightless** for a day.

wild

A **wild** animal finds its own food.

winter

It snowed this **winter**.

wondered

Pete **wondered** if he spelled the word correctly.

would

I **would** like to eat lunch before we play.

Yy

yellow

The ducklings are all **yellow**.

Acknowledgments

The publisher gratefully acknowledges permission to reprint the following copyrighted material:

"Gray Goose" from *Yellow Elephant: A Bright Bestiary* by Julie Larios, paintings by Julie Paschkis. Text copyright © 2006 by Julie Larios. Illustrations copyright © 2006 by Julie Paschkis. Reprinted by permission of Houghton Mifflin Harcourt Publishing Company.

"Happy Fall" from *Pinwheel Days* by Ellen Tarlow, illustrations by Gretel Parker. Text copyright © 2007 by Ellen Tarlow. Illustrations copyright © 2007 by Gretel Parker. Used by permission of Star Bright Books, Inc.

Kitten's First Full Moon by Kevin Henkes. Copyright © 2004 by Kevin Henkes. Used by permission of Greenwillow Books, an imprint of HarperCollins.

A Tiger Cub Grows Up by Joan Hewett, photographed by Richard Hewett. Text copyright © 2002 by Joan Hewett. Photographs copyright © 2002 by Richard Hewett. Reprinted by permission of Carolrhoda Books, Inc., a division of Lerner Publishing Group.

Book Cover, A HARBOR SEAL PUP GROWS UP by Joan Hewett, photographs by Richard Hewett. Text copyright © 2001 by Joan Hewett. Photographs copyright © 2001 by Richard Hewett. Reprinted by permission of Carolrhoda Books, Inc., a division of Lerner Publishing Group.

Book Cover, A PENGUIN CHICK GROWS UP by Joan Hewett, photographs by Richard Hewett. Text copyright © 2004 by Joan Hewett. Photographs copyright © 2004 by Richard Hewett. Reprinted by permission of Carolrhoda Books, Inc., a division of Lerner Publishing Group.

ILLUSTRATIONS
Cover Illustration: Pablo Bernasconi

8–9: Constanza Basaluzzo. 10–43: Kevin Henkes. 44–49: John Kaufmann. 56–75: John Kanzler. 100–101: Lizzy Rockwell. 102–117: Gretel Parker. 124: Ken Bowser. 129: Tom Leonard. 156–157: Julie Paschkis. 160–161: Melissa Sweet.

PHOTOGRAPHY
All photographs are by Ken Cavanagh or Ken Karp for Macmillan/McGraw Hill (MMH) except as noted below.

iv: Ann Cutting/Jupiter Images. v: (t) Panoramic Images/Getty Images; (b) Richard Hewitt. 2–3: Ann Cutting/Jupiter Images. 4: Scott W. Smith/Animals Animals. 4–5: (bkgd-moss & stream) Digital Archive Japan/Alamy; (ferns) Comstock Images/Alamy. 5: Altrendo Travel/Getty Images. 6–7: Richard Broadwell/Alamy. 44–46: NASA. 47: Dorling Kindersley. 48: NASA. 49: NASA Kennedy Space Center. 50: image 100/PunchStock. 51: Bill Brooks/Masterfile. 52–53: Jose Luis Pelaez, Inc./Corbis. 54–55: Ken Cavanagh/Macmillan/McGraw-Hill. 74: Courtesy of Phillip Dray. 76: Ken Cavanagh/Macmillan/McGraw-Hill. 77: (c) Andrew Syred/Science Photo Library/Photo Researchers; (cr) Davies & Starr/Getty Images. 78: (tl) Steve Gschmeissner/Photo Researchers; (br) Stephen Marks/Getty Images. 79: (tl) Dennis Kunkel/Phototake; (tr) David Sacks/Getty Images. 80: Bananastock/Imagestate. 81: Philadelphia Museum of Art/Corbis. 82–83: Panoramic Images/Getty Images. 84: Derek Davies/Getty Images. 85: (bkgd) C Squared Studios/Getty Images; (t) Wisconsin State Journal/John Maniaci/AP Images. 86: Jim Cummins/Getty Images. 87: Peter N. Fox/AGE Fotostock. 88: John Henshall/Alamy. 89: (c) Jim Reed/Photo Researchers; (inset) Jim Reed/Photo Researchers. 89: Stockbyte/Punchstock. 90: AP Images. 91: (t) Warren Faidley/Corbis; (cr) Reuters/Jeff Mitchell/Newscom. 92: (tr) Richard Hutchings/Photo Edit; (cl) David Hanover/Getty Images. 92–93: DAJ/Getty Images. 96: Comstock/Jupiter Images. 97: (bc) Bet Noire/Shutterstock; (br) C Squared Studios/Getty Images. 98–99: (bkgd) Bonnie Nance/Dembinsky Photo Associates. 116: (tr) Ken Cavanagh; (cr) Courtesy of Gretel Parker. 118–119: (bkgd) Ariel Skelley/Getty Images. 119: (b) Jan Halaska/Photo Researchers. 120: (bkgd) Comstock/Punchstock; (b) Jan Halaska/Photo Researchers. 121: (t) Comstock/Punchstock; (b) Jan Halaska/Photo Researchers. 122: (bkgd) Blend Images/Punchstock; (b) Jan Halaska/Photo Researchers. 123: Jan Halaska/Photo Researchers. 124: Dick Luria/Getty Images. 125: D. Hurst/Alamy. 126–127: Tom Murphy/National Geographic Image Collection. 128: Carl R. Sams II/Peter Arnold, Inc. 131–153: Richard Hewitt. 154: (tl) Joan Hewett. 154–155: Richard Hewitt. 158: Michael Newman/Photo Edit. 15: Arthur Tilley/Getty Images. 162: (cl) Digital Archive Japan/Alamy; (c) Rainman/Zefa/Corbis; (cr) Royalty-Free/Corbis; (bl) Frank Krahmer/Masterfile; (br) Jim Reed/Corbis. 163: (l to r) Digital Archive Japan/Alamy; Rainman/Zefa/Corbis; Royalty-Free/Corbis; Frank Krahmer/Masterfile; Jim Reed/Corbis. 165: (tr) Ken Karp/Macmillan McGraw-Hill. 166: (cr) Jeremy Woodhouse/Masterfile; (bl) Denis Scott/Corbis. 167: (t) Royalty-Free/Corbis; (b) Masterfile Royalty Free. 168: Jack Hollingsworth/Getty Images. 169: Jeremy Woodhouse/Masterfile. 170: (t) Yann Arthus-Bertrand/Corbis; (b) Timothy Shonnard/Getty Images. 171: Joseph Sohm; ChromoSohm Inc./Corbis. 172: Layne Kennedy/Corbis. 173: Royalty-Free/Corbis. 173: Ryan McVay/Getty Images. 174: Masterfile Royalty Free. 174: Denis Scott/Corbis. 175: David Joel/Getty Images. 176: Rommel/Masterfile. 177: Image Source/Getty Images.